John (Phrenologist) Thompson

Phrenology and its uses

embracing the choice of pursuits, good health, how to save money, and how to

make life a success

John (Phrenologist) Thompson

Phrenology and its uses
embracing the choice of pursuits, good health, how to save money, and how to make life a success

ISBN/EAN: 9783741155222

Manufactured in Europe, USA, Canada, Australia, Japa

Cover: Foto ©Andreas Hilbeck / pixelio.de

Manufactured and distributed by brebook publishing software (www.brebook.com)

John (Phrenologist) Thompson

Phrenology and its uses

PHRENOLOGY and ITS USES:

EMBRACING

THE CHOICE OF PURSUITS,

GOOD HEALTH,

HOW TO SAVE MONEY,

AND

HOW TO MAKE LIFE A SUCCESS.

BY

JOHN THOMPSON,

Author of "Body, Brain, and Mind," "Man's Sexual Relations,"
"Facts About Tobacco," "How to Remember: or, The Art of Never Forgetting,"
"Love and Matrimony," "Tight Lacing and Other Fallacies,"
and several other Works on Mental Science, Health, etc.

PUBLISHED BY THE AUTHOR AT

BROUGHTON HOUSE, SOUTH CLIFF, SCARBORO'.

of intellect, domestic happiness, home enjoyments, moral excellence, and, of course, pecuniary sufficiency, or enough money to make us independent in old age.

It should be remembered, in considering our needs of money, that, though often our wants may appear many, our real needs are few. Too often those who possess the most money make a vicious use of it, and, instead of turning it to the good of humanity, they gratify a few pampered and sinful desires. Such people necessarily live a mean and selfish life, which is always an unhappy one. In like manner, when very wonderful talents are misused, they make their owners' lives miserable failures.

Julius Cæsar was a man of extraordinary abilities, and was undoubtedly successful in his efforts; but we cannot look upon his *life* as a brilliant success. Napoleon Bonaparte was similarly endowed and, for a time, seemed marvellously successful in all his undertakings. He made a greater stir than any man who ever ruled in Europe; but his ambition overstepped its legitimate bounds and brought the whole fabric of his aspirations crumbling at the foot of England, sent him into exile, and cut short the length of his days. Captain Webb was the greatest aquatic performer in the world; but, in endeavouring to extend his exalted position, he ventured on the mad expedition which resulted in his destruction. Fred Archer was the greatest jockey in the world. His efforts were crowned with remarkable success; but in none of these cases can we see the elements of genuine success.

The man who has a million of money, but does not enjoy good health and peace of mind, is poor indeed; while the man who has nothing besides that for which he works hard, if he has good health and enjoys his work, is well to do; yea! he is infinitely richer than the millionaire, who has not health to enjoy his plenty.

The contented business man, who enjoys good health and length of days, is in a more enviable position than either a Cæsar or a Napoleon.

The same law applies to intellect, home, affection, and business, and to every other position occupied by man, and every condition in which he is placed. The normal action of every faculty of the mind confers pleasure, and in no other way can this pleasure be enjoyed than by their legitimate exercise. Men make their own misery, by sacrificing all their higher and nobler faculties on the altar of the god of money; they sordidly try to get rich in worldly goods. Their sole end and aim in this life appear to be the accumulation of property; and, as a consequence, their social nature starves, their moral principles get warped and perverted, and all their capacities for substantial enjoyment are seriously diminished, if not absolutely annihilated.

CHAPTER II.

VARIETIES OF AMBITION.

WE are sometimes inclined to consider the life of a man successful when he has accomplished the object of his ambition; but in doing so we make a mistake. A man, who gets all he desires in this life, may consider himself successful, but his idea of life and good things may be so imperfect that, viewed from a higher platform, what he considers success may be blank failure. Men's opinions of success in life differ according to their organizations. Men look at life through coloured glasses, as it were, and, although it is computed that hundreds of thousands of millions of human beings have lived since the creation of man, it is most probable that not even two of that vast multitude have looked through glasses of the same shade of colour; or, in other words, so diversified is human character that no two have ever viewed life and success from the same standpoint.

It is marvellous how varied we find man's ambition. It governs every variety of human effort and achievement. It is an element that we find existing in all spheres of life, from the beggar to the king; from the thief to the judge; from the Sunday school teacher to the bishop; from the rag collector to the shop-owner or merchant; from the pugilist to the philanthropist. Some are anxious to be one thing, some another. Scholars, scientists, statesmen, soldiers, preachers, explorers, rulers, etc.,—all vie with their contemporaries for the lead in their professions.

Burning with this sentiment, we have Capt. Webb in the swimming art; Fred Archer as a jockey; John L. Sullivan in the ring; Brigham Young in polygamy; Charles Peace in house-breaking; and many an one of each of those, and others on a smaller scale.

Each of the persons we have mentioned may have secured in this life the position for which the natural bent of his mind, and the influence of his surroundings, inclined him, yet may have neglected many conditions essential to true success. The phrenologist measures a man's success by the use he makes of the powers given him; and when the affairs of human life come to be looked over by the Great Auditor, we think that a man's success in life will greatly depend upon the preparation he has made here for his future state.

Let each of my readers see well to the cultivation of their entire natures, and stick to whatever plough they put their hands, nor turn, nor look back, but prosecute their work with a singleness of purpose, and nobleness of aim worthy of beings made in the image and likeness of God.

Reader, choose that work, the execution of which will conduce, not only to your own, but also to the welfare of humanity at large. You can then be justified in throwing your whole soul and energy into it.

CHAPTER III.

PHRENOLOGY.

PHRENOLOGY is the great key that unlocks the doorway to success and happiness, or to true riches. It is the handmaid of Christianity, and one of the greatest helps to individual and human improvement placed within the reach of man. It shows clearly what powers are possessed by every man. It teaches those who are defective wherein they are so, and how they may overcome their weaknesses; in short, it reveals every virtue and vice, power and defect, even the motive springs of our every action, and lays bare every attribute and idiosyncrasy peculiar to each. There is no other thing in the world which will so effectually enable man to understand both others and himself as this glorious science. If men only knew the hundredth part of its value, they would embrace it as their dearest and best friend; they would eagerly grasp the morals of its precious teachings, and imbibe its principles as their infallible guide in nearly everything appertaining to this life, and much that would be beneficial for the future. Phrenology, as we teach it to-day, is " The Science of Man" in every sense of the word, because it deals with every part of man.

When a boy is sent to school the teacher is considered

to have done his duty when he has taught the child how to read, write, cipher, spell, and speak English properly, or when he has trained it so that it can pass the necessary examinations properly.

The physician thinks he has done his duty when he has alleviated pain and established physical health, and so he rests satisfied.

The lawyer is conscious of having performed his part in the great drama of life when he has rectified wrongs, restored peace and order, and established justice.

The minister, who is the ordained watchman on the tower of morality, is looked upon as having performed his duty well when he has warned us against moral sins and provided good food for our religious nature. And so it is in every other profession. Men are in the main specialists, attending only to one or two parts of man's nature; administering to only one or two of his multifarious requirements. But it is otherwise with the phrenologist. His duty is to warn men against every form of sin, whether of a moral or a physical nature; to persuade men to give up injurious habits; to instruct them in the laws of life and health, and to show them how to establish and retain health both of body and mind. It is also his duty to point out their mental excesses and deficiencies, their moral weaknesses and selfishness, and to show how they may overcome these defects—how to strengthen the one and regulate the other. Also to tell people how to choose companions suitable for them, so that they may live in harmony, peace, happiness, and usefulness; to point out to those who do not live happily together how to understand each other; to instruct parents how to train up their children so as to make them useful members of society, a blessing to themselves, and an honour to the community to which they belong; and lastly, but by no means of the least importance, it is his duty to tell people for what they are mentally and physically adapted, or in what profession, business, or field of industry they will be the most successful, most happy, and most useful. This is the object of this work, and that it may be helpful in guiding many to success in life is the sincere desire of the author.

The phrenologist's work is not one of idly entertaining people or catering to their sense of the ridiculous and making them laugh, although he may sometimes gratify the faculty of Mirthfulness; but his mission is to instruct the people in a science which is calculated, if properly applied, to lift man to an infinitely higher standard of moral excellence, intellectual attainment, social felicity, and physical health than he has ever acquired.

Phrenology does not profess to teach theology save to establish, by showing the existence of natural mental faculties, that man is a religious being; but it brings man to the point of education where he is best adapted to receive theological instruction. The work of the phrenologist is to educate men in the truest sense of the word; to help them to improve time, talents, and health; in short, to improve and economise life. To become rich in the sense I have explained,—rich in morals, in intellect, in social enjoyments, in health of body and mind, in pecuniary affairs, and in general usefulness—rich in love for God, as manifested in doing His will, and in obeying His Divine laws.

Speaking of this science, the Hon. John Neal says :—"If we would know the truth of ourselves, we must interrogate phrenology, and follow out her teachings, as we would a course of religious training, after we had once become satisfied of its truth. . . . The result of all my experience for something over two score years is this : that phrenology is a revelation put by God himself within the reach of all His intelligent creation, to be studied and applied in all the relations and in all the business of life."

And the Rev. Henry Ward Beecher says :—"All my life long I have been in the habit of using phrenology as that which solves the practical phenomena of life. I regard it as far more useful, practical, and sensible than any other system of mental philosophy which has yet been evolved. Certainly phrenology has introduced mental philosophy to the common people."

Horace Mann says :—" I declare myself a hundred times more indebted to phrenology than to all the metaphysical works I ever read. . . . I look upon phrenology as the guide to philosophy, and the handmaid of Christianity. Whoever disseminates true phrenology is a public benefactor."

CHAPTER IV.

TIME AND TALENTS.

IT is a sad fact that men and women waste their time in numerous different ways for want of instruction, and for want of thought. Perhaps few of us think enough about the value of time, although it is of infinite importance to us all. When we think about the time measured out to us, it appears but short: yea, it is very short. Longfellow, in his " Psalm of Life," says :—

> "Art is long, and time is fleeting,
> And our hearts, though stout and brave,
> Still like muffled drums are beating
> Funeral marches to the grave."

This is true, and it behoves us to be up and doing. We should utilize every moment; each day we should try to learn and do something which will advance us to a higher level of life.

Some men have been wonderful economisers of time, and have accomplished great works by utilizing their spare moments.

Elihu Burritt, while earning his living as a blacksmith, learned eighteen languages and twenty-two dialects by simply utilizing odd moments.

Kirke White learned Greek while walking too and from a lawyer's office.

Dr. Darwin compiled nearly all his works while riding in a carriage, writing his thoughts in a memorandum book which he carried for the purpose.

And how much could not some of my readers have accomplished if they had put to a good use all the precious moments they have carelessly squandered? If you waste but one hour per day it amounts to fifteen days in a year, or a whole year in twenty-four. Some men have looked upon time as being money. The great and wealthy Rothschild said, "time is money to me." Yet some men waste their time in lounging about the streets, sitting smoking and drinking in public-houses, and talking gossip. Many would rather do this than read a useful book. Some waste their time in gambling, card playing, and in dog and horse-racing. Women sometimes waste their time in talking scandal about their neighbours ; and there are thousands of both men and women who waste their time, and energy too, in working at occupations for which they have no natural aptitude.

Men have fought hard and long trying to overcome difficulties,—have studied hard, both early in the morning and late at night, trying to master their profession ; and, after spending their time, their money, their energy, in short, their all, have miserably failed, and, broken-hearted, have sunk into the grave. These were men who were well-endowed, and might have shone like stars in society, and grown wealthy in prosecuting some trade or profession, but because they were put to the wrong thing their life was a failure.

We have been speaking about waste of time; does not this involve waste of talents? Of course it does. Every man has talents, more or less, which, if legitimately exercised, or put to good account, would secure for him respectability, and a full share of success. But, as Shakespeare says—"There is a tide in the affairs of men, which, when taken at the flood, leads on to fortune. Omitted, all the voyage of their life is bound in shallows and in miseries." Men who work at vocations for which they are not adapted omit taking the tide at its flood; they waste their talents, and often ruin their health, blight their happiness, destroy their peace of mind, and bring on permanent old age, and sometimes disease and death.

CHAPTER V.

CHOICE OF PURSUITS.

THE one great thought that occupies the mind of every thoughtful boy who is at school, or about to leave it, is the vocation he must pursue in after life. Many serious mistakes have been made, and are still being made, in this momentous matter, owing to a want of that knowledge which phrenology imparts. The majority of young people are totally ignorant of their abilities and equally so of their inefficiencies. Not having had the advantages of that great teacher experience, they are frequently led away by a blind fancy, or are forced by parents who are equally ignorant, or perhaps by sheer necessity, to serve an apprenticeship to a trade or profession for which they are not by nature adapted, and which they never can enjoy. Some parents have the idea that the boy should be allowed to have his own choice in the matter of a trade or profession ; but this is allowing the boy to make a dangerous experiment. It is impossible for him to have any bias on which to found his choice, except that of mere fancy, and this, at the best, is a very cruel guide. Every person of experience knows that the boy frequently takes a dozen different fancies, and perhaps in none of them does he choose a vocation for which his abilities fit him. If parents allow their children to be guided in the choice of a vocation in this way, they submit their children to blind chance, or make life a success like the result of a lottery. They cannot be certain of any result, good or bad. When such have served their apprenticeship and come to battle with the world, and make headway for themselves, they find out their mistake. But not until they have wasted the best years of their existence; not until their wealth and energy have been spent in trying to accomplish an impossibility. A few such individuals by repeated experiments find out for what they are adapted, and perhaps succeed to some extent; but the great majority struggle on in poverty, or losing all hope and ambition, they sink into a life of shame, crime, and ruin.

Not only is this state of affairs derogatory to the individual who has made the mistake, but it is a very prolific cause of mischief to the community at large. Much of the drunkenness, criminality, and pauperism that scourge and burden our country are caused by the wrong choice of life-pursuits.

Respectable, well-bred, and well-educated men and women are thus reduced to sheer poverty, and are forced from respectability and salubrious localities to begging, if not criminality and the city slum. Their children are reared in such homes as the following lines describe :—

> Each house is many storeys high,
> Each room a family contains ;
> And there they breed, and breathe foul air,
> Like rats inhabiting the drains.

Though when one comes to think of it,
   The rats are far more clean and sweet;
These people neither comb nor wash,
   Rats trim their fur and keep it neat.

Oh, dear! oh, dear! the sights one sees,
   In a close court, the other day;
I saw some lean, large-stomached babies,
   All busy at their childish play.

They dabbled in the thick, black slime,
   Stuck fish heads in and drew them out,
Made pies of stuff much worse than mud,
   While fat blue-bottles buzzed about.

Poor innocents! for those who die
   In early years, what bliss untold,
To pass from filth and haddock heads!
   To seas of glass and streets of gold!

On the other hand, if the principles and teachings of phrenology were thoroughly understood and put into practice, much of the crime and wretchedness, which now exist and scourge our country, would be banished, for there would be more success and less failure. Every man would be placed in his right sphere. The natural mechanic would be in the workshop, the farmer would follow the plough, the merchant would be in the store, the artist in the studio, the preacher in the pulpit, the statesman in the halls of legislature; in short, every man would be placed in his natural sphere, and this being the case, each man would be in possession of means that would secure for him the very highest success and enjoyment that he is capable of either securing or enjoying. There would be no fear

B

of him failing provided he was industrious and attended to the conditions necessary to success, for phrenology would tell him plainly what his abilities and deficiencies were, and would point out means by which he could improve and perfect himself.

It must be remembered, however, that there are certain conditions essential to success with which every man must comply. These conditions will be treated on in another chapter. Another great mistake that young people make is in aspiring to a high and responsible position at first, and in wishing to start at the top of the ladder instead of the foot. It is best to start humbly, at a humble post, and by dint of integrity and perseverance, rise to the position you wish to attain. " He that exalteth himself shall be abased, but he that humbleth himself shall be exalted."

Many young men are ambitious to become merchants, ministers, doctors, lawyers, artists, and engineers, when really they are better adapted for farming, mechanism, and the simpler branches of industry. Many parents are equally to blame in being over ambitious for their children. It is far better to fill a humble vocation well than an exalted one badly—to be a good mechanic or a good farmer, than a bad preacher or a bungling doctor. And besides this, there are far more chances of success in farming or mechanics than there are in the professions. We want nearly five hundred mechanics and farmers to one professional man. At the present time, owing to the peculiar ideas of parents and young people, nearly every profession and business is swarming with aspirants to wealth and fame, while farming is neglected. Some young men are to blame themselves, but the majority, I believe, are sent into these professions by their excessively conceited and ambitious parents, who wish their sons to earn their livelihood easily, or who desire them to move in better society than has been the case with themselves. In business many of our large houses are overcrowded with assistants, and thousands cannot get employment. In watching the times we find that every mercantile change has a great deal to do with the morality of individuals. Because young men are expected to appear respectable, and because they are fond of dress, theatre going, and other amusements, and are expected to spend money freely, smoke cigars, drink wine, and bet occasionally, which are all far too expensive luxuries for their income, they are tempted to commit frauds. They embezzle their masters' money, and then abscond. I have known several young men, who have done this, to be imprisoned and punished severely for their misconduct, and never afterwards able to secure a good position. Others, I have known, who have fled from the country to avoid disgrace, and thus lost comfortable homes and loving friends for ever. This ought to be a good reason why every young man should think seriously before he aspires to be a merchant. Becoming a merchant at the present time is like entering a lottery, where, for each one hundred blanks there is only one prize. And the same may be said of the professions.

On the other hand, farming and mechanics provide abundant fields for the exercise of excellent talents and the acquisition of wealth. There are millions of acres of land in India, Africa, Australia, New Zealand, and America, rich in every variety of fruits and vegetables, the soil and climate suitable for roots and grains, rich also in minerals of every kind, with no one to gather and enjoy their inexhaustible stores. The few enterprising persons who have gone out and taken possession of and cultivated small tracts of land in these countries are now well to do. Some have come home to the "mother country" in the possession of large fortunes. And anyone of industrious habits and natural abilities may yet go there and make themselves independent. It would be better to emigrate than starve, better to go to those wide fields of effort and of wealth, than live here on a mere pittance, barely sufficient to keep body and soul together. I am not in favour of emigration further than is necessary, and I believe that it would be better for many people if they would unite in limiting the increase of our population within the country's means of sustenance. Readers who desire to have special information on this particular point are referred to the work on "Man's Sexual Relations."

With these few hints I will pass on to show that persons differ in their capacity to learn different trades. A person's ability to learn depends upon his various phrenological developments. One may be able to learn arithmetic very quickly, and will be very dull at reading and spelling; and *vice versa.* Another may be able to draw, but not able to arrange and combine colours ; while some are imperfect drawers and good painters. Some people have a great thirst for travelling, and ability for the study of geography and navigation, and can remember most distinctly where they saw things last and the roads they once traversed. They can find their way to places almost intuitively, or as if by instinct, and remember the streets in large cities, but are unable to remember events and dates. The Rev. W. Dunn, Congregational Minister (who is much respected by all who know him), has a good memory for events and can calculate very rapidly, but he cannot remember localities, and frequently loses himself in towns he has visited for more than a dozen times. Some people are good in their perceptive faculties, practical and of a matter-of-fact turn of mind, but are unable to plan and contrive, and their inventive talent is poor. Others again are all theory ; they can plan, scheme, invent new ways of doing things, and lay out work for others, but are dull in their perceptives and lack practical talent. Some are forcible, energetic, persevering, tenacious, and hard to overcome ; while others are tame, irresolute, and lacking in executive power. Some have good mechanical abilities, and can construct almost anything, but are poor talkers. In short, every person can be a genius in one thing and very dull in another. Some people are successful in everything they turn their hands to ; they are well developed in every faculty, and can learn one thing about as easily as another. While others are dull in everything, have many ups and downs in life, and what they gain is by the most protracted and laborious effort.

Phrenology reveals this great mystery of the mind, and opens to all parents two important considerations. First, it shows what children and youths can best learn and in what they can gain the highest amount of success. Second, it points out their weaknesses, and, therefore, what needs special cultivation. And, what is more, it tells parents how to assist their children in strengthening their weaknesses and perfecting their characters. Some information on this point will be found in " The Art of Never Forgetting." If parents would either study and apply the teachings of phrenology themselves, or consult some reliable phrenologist respecting the talents of their children, prior to putting them to a trade or profession, they would obviate much, if not all, the misery and mischief resulting from a wrong choice of pursuit. They would also obtain for their children facilities for gaining the highest amount of success their talents are capable of. For the instruction of those who may have studied books on phrenology, but more especially parents, and to awaken a disposition to study more carefully this important matter, I will point out the phrenological development and physiological conditions required for the successful prosecution of a number of common vocations.

CHAPTER VI.

MECHANICAL TRADES.

I MENTION these trades first, because we need more men in these classes of industry than in any other. Just think how many men it takes to build a house, not to mention filling it with all kinds of furniture, pictures, pottery, cutlery, cooking utensils, clothing, jewellry, and a variety of other things. We need first of all the labourer, bricklayer, stonemason, plasterer, carpenter, glazier, slater, smith, brass-workers, and a number more before the house is fit to be occupied. Even in clothing our person we need a number of mechanics; first of all, the weaver, and in this industry there is no end of variety. Also the button maker, boot and shoe makers, stocking knitters, glove manufacturers, tailors, hatters, and others besides. When we think of building and furnishing a house, and clothing the family, as well as the manufacture of tools for every conceivable workmanship such as are used in the building of ships, guns, agricultural implements, carriages, locomotives, and spinning and weaving machinery, one might think that three-fourths of the human family were employed as mechanics. In fact, to build and furnish a house we need the assistance of nearly fifty different classes of mechanics;

and if we take into account the the clothing of the family the number runs up to over a hundred.

The mechanic has more to do with securing our comfort and convenience than any other individual. We are dependent upon him more than on any one else. His work is as honourable as any other, and requires considerable talent. Some branches of mechanics require the highest order of intellect that man can manifest. Making printing, sewing, and knitting machines is no child's play; constructing clocks, watches, and jewellery requires the most skilful workmanship. It requires ingenuity to manufacture cloth and make garments. In fact, when we think about all the comforts, conveniences, and refinements of life, the mechanic seems to be one of the most important men of the community. This wide field of usefulness embraces trades requiring almost every variety of talent, from the man who makes wash tubs to the man who builds magnificent steamships, to carry passengers to different parts of the world.

The question here naturally arises, what qualities are required to ensure success in these capacities? All mechanics need Constructiveness and the perceptives, but especially Form, Size, Weight, and Order. They should also possess a fair degree of Causality to give planning power, and Destructiveness and Combativeness to give spirit, force, executive power, and the disposition to fight with difficulties. These developments give a particular shape to the head; the lower part of the forehead is prominent, the temples well rounded out, and the head rather broad in the region of the ears. The portrait of Sir William G. Armstrong, though not very correctly representing his present appearance, is a good illustration of the successful mechanic, and shows those very developments already mentioned. The heavier branches of mechanics, such as stonemasonry, bricklaying, blacksmithing, shipbuilding, car-

Fig. 1.—Sir W. G. Armstrong.

pentry, and most of the branches included in the manufacture of heavy tools and machinery, require a large development of the bones and muscles to give strength, toughness, and endurance ; and these must be supported by a good development of the organs which manufacture vitality, or, in other words, there must be a good development of the Motive and Vital Temperaments. For an explanation of the Temperaments the reader is here referred to the appendix. The lighter branches of mechanics, such as manufacturing cloth, paper, cutlery, nails, pins, etc., as also bookbinding, printing, engraving, picture-frame-making, tailoring, pen-making, and watch-making, require activity; hence, men in these branches need more sensitive nerves, which come from an active Mental Temperament and a fair degree of the Vital. In these occupations men of small stature, and those with slender bodies, may find employment, and succeed often better than big men. In other respects, the better phrenological and physiological developments the mechanic possesses, the better it will be for him under all circumstances. He will enjoy life better, and do more good to his fellow-men if he has strong social feelings, a high moral nature, a powerful intellect, and ability to express himself fluently.

In my personal experience I have come in contact with a number of young men who have been ambitious to become engineers, and not a few fond parents are anxious that their sons may distinguish themselves in this line of mechanics. I fear that both parents and young men omit looking at the actual facts relating to engineering life. Though the engineer requires more of the Mental than of the Physical Temperament, he has at first all the drudgery work to do, which is rough, hard, and uncongenial to a soft, pleasure-loving nature. When this is done, and a thorough acquaintance with the work has been made, the man's success depends entirely on his abilities. As there are few master engineers required, few only can rise to distinction. Chances of promotion are only perhaps one in ten, and the probability is that the man may have to do hard engineering work all his days.

The different branches of engineering work require different talents. The civil and military engineer must have good reasoning powers, so as to plan railways, canals, tunnels, bridges, etc. Chemistry and mathematics must be studied so as to comprehend the nature or quality of the materials he uses, and so as to determine the laws of gravity, force, and resistance. In this branch the organs of Causality, Comparison, Eventuality, Form, Size, Weight, Order, Calculation, Constructiveness, Firmness, Destructiveness, and Combativeness, should all be large. This combination is well illustrated in Mark I. Brunel, who was one of the most successful engineers that ever lived. His head is well rounded out in nearly every particular, and is also large. He had a healthy physiology, and would have been successful in almost any branch of the world's industry, or in nearly any department of the world's great workshop.

Mechanical and agricultural engineering refers to machinery, steam engines, etc. The man who desires to follow either of these pursuits should possess large Constructiveness, Calculation, Form, Size, Weight, Order, Causality, and Comparison. He also needs a good memory for dates and events, so as to remember all the details connected with engineering work. He should possess a good degree of Destructiveness and Firmness, to give force, executiveness, and perseverance; in short, to do all kinds of engineering well, it requires, first and last, nearly all there is of a man, however exalted his talents or extended his culture.

The engraver having finer work to do than the engineer, should have a finer Temperament, large Ideality, Order, Constructiveness, Form, and Comparison. He needs less

Fig. 2.—Mark I. Brunel.

Destructiveness and Combativeness than the engineer, and a predominance of the Mental Temperament.

In the realm of mechanics there are numerous suitable employments for women, but those mostly fulfilled by them are dressmaking and millinery.

Dressmakers should · have the organs of Form, Size,

Weight, Colour, Order, Constructiveness, and Ideality, well developed with a predominance of the Mental-Vital Temperament. Those with dark complexions are better suited for the work than fair ones.

Milliners need large Colour, Ideality, Form, Size, Order, and Constructiveness, and in other respects the same as the dressmaker.

CHAPTER VII.

AGRICULTURAL PURSUITS.

FARMING in this country has of late years sunk seriously in the estimation of the people. Owing to the importation of foreign provisions, cattle, etc., and to the higher rents, it has not been remunerative ; and on this account hundreds of people, who have been bred to agricultural work, have left it for city life. Yet farming, when rightly done, is one of the finest, most healthful, and enjoyable of occupations. And we want quite twice as many farmers as there are in England to-day, because extensive farmers do not cultivate the land properly. Part of it is being continually neglected. Small farmers manage their land the best, and produce the most, and proportionately make the most money. England would produce twice as much grain, vegetables, and fruit as it does now, if it were divided into small farms and properly cultivated. The causes of much poverty and destitution among farmers to-day are discoverable in the fact that they are imperfectly educated. By far the majority never read books on, or study, either chemistry, physiology, botany, or any other of the sciences, a knowledge of which would conduce to their success. If they would study chemistry, they would then be able to understand the nature of soils and manures, and their adaptation to each other. If they would study physiology, they might be able to understand the laws of health, and would also, in most cases, be able to doctor their own cattle.   And botany should have their attention, so that they may understand the nature of vegetables, fruits, and grains.   It is not muscular force that the farmer needs altogether ; he should prosecute his vocation intelligently, instead of trying to do things by brute force alone. The intelligent farmer always get his work done better and with less expense than the ignorant one, though the latter may be much the stronger physically, and have about him men of like bodily proportions.   The farmer does not need as much refinement and blandness of manners as the merchant or minister; but we believe, when found with these qualities, he would be a more perfect man and a better farmer.

I have known farmers of the old school complain seriously because their sons were fond of reading and studying. This is a great mistake, for such sons, if allowed to study, are sure to outstrip their fathers in the successful prosecution of their pursuit.   The farmer requires a strong body to keep him healthy and vigorous.   He needs a full degree of the Motive Temperament to give toughness and endurance, and the Vital Temperament sufficient to give good nutritive and sustaining power ; large Combativeness and Destructiveness to give force and industry, Cautiousness and Acquisitiveness to give prudence and economy, and Constructiveness to be able to use tools and understand machinery.   He also needs large perceptive faculties to give judgment of cattle and work, a good memory to store up facts and past experience for use in the future, and strong domestic feelings to make him care for his flocks and herds. The accompanying portrait of Andrew Mc.Kenzie illustrates the developments required by the farmer. Mr. Mc.Kenzie was born of poor parents, and reared in poverty and hardship. By dint of industry and economy he saved

Fig. 3.—Mr. Andrew Mc.Kenzie.

as much money as enabled him to take a farm, which he has carried on successfully for many years, and is now in a position to live independently. The gardener may be said to be a farmer on a small scale, and he needs almost precisely the same qualities as a farmer. He must have good muscular strength, practical talent, and domestic feelings, with a higher development of Ideality than is essential in the farmer. Perhaps this is the only difference necessary.

CHAPTER VIII

MERCANTILE PURSUITS.

IN this occupation we have all sorts, from the man who gathers rags and bones, old boots and shoes, from house to house, wheeling a handcart, or carrying a sack in which to convey his merchandise, to the man who sends ships to India and China for silks and teas. Many young men think it desirable to be called "a merchant." I wonder what kind of merchants they wonld like to be. There is certainly any amount of choice for them. Variety of trades demands almost an equal variety of talents. There are grocers, drapers, ironmongers, wood merchants, wool merchants, grain merchants, spirit merchants, tobacco merchants, fruit, fish, and chip potato merchants.

Grocers need a full degree of the Motive Temperament, and a large degree of the Vital, large perceptive organs, and a bland, agreeable, social nature. They ought to be good tempered, because they have to put up with a good deal of insolence from customers.

Drapers need more of the Mental Temperament, with large Ideality, Colour, Order, and Approbativeness.

Ironmongers ought to be natural mechanics, so as to understand the articles they sell. Men with dark hair are better adapted for ironmongers than those of light complexions.

C

Wood, wool, and grain merchants need a full degree of
Physical Temperaments, combined with keen perceptives,
and a broad head to give push and energy.

A bookseller needs a full degree of the literary faculties;
these are Eventuality, Locality, Language, and Time, and a

Fig. 4—George Moore.

liberal development of the Mental Temperament, to give a
studious nature and a love for reading.   I have observed
that men who acquire a general knowledge of the books
they have to sell succeed the best.

Canvassers need the Vital Temperament, large Language,
Human Nature, Eventuality, Firmness, Acquisitiveness,
Mirthfulness, Agreeableness, and Friendship.   In other
respects they should be like the bookseller.

For office work one should have large perceptives, an active Temperament, Benevolence, Veneration, and Conscientiousness, so as to be sharp, active, respectful, and honest. Fig. 4 represents a very successful merchant. From a poor boy, in the meanest place in the establishment, he rose to be the head of one of the largest mercantile houses in London. From poverty he rose to wealth. He was a man of energy of character; nothing could turn him aside from his purpose. He was fond of bargaining and making money; but was at the same time liberal-minded and just.

CHAPTER IX

LITERARY CALLINGS.

IN those who do literary work a preponderance of the Mental Temperament is always desirable. It is chiefly the brain that has the work to do, not their arms or

Fig. 5—The Rev. Charles Garrett.

legs; but the stronger and healthier their bodies are the better. In the portraits used to illustrate different literary requirements, it will be seen that each has a good degree of the Physical Temperaments.

A clergyman requires the Mental-Vital Temperament to give mental clearness and enthusiasm; the moral organs large, to exercise an elevating influence over his fellow-men; Acquisitiveness to make him economical; the literary faculties to make him fond of study, and to give power to impart information; large Comparison, Human Nature, and Agreeableness; in short, a clergyman ought to be as near a perfect man as possible, and especially ought a preacher to be free from every bad habit. A clergyman who either

Fig. 6—Archdeacon Farrar.

smokes tobacco or drinks spirits should be looked upon as an abomination. A man who smokes is not fit to minister to the spiritual needs of the people. His example will be bad. Children are very imitiative creatures, and, when they see men smoke and drink, especially if those men are looked upon as good by their elders, are anxious to follow their example, and become like them.

The schoolmaster is a kind of minister, and should possess the same qualities as a clergyman, with large Parental Love, and should also avoid bad habits.

The Rev. Charles Garrett, ex-President of the Wesleyan Conference, very fairly illustrates the developments suit-

Fig. 7—William Wordsworth.

able for a clergyman. He is noted for his deep sympathies, and his earnest endeavours to enlighten the ignorant, and benefit the poor. He is much loved and admired by all who know him, but especially by poor people.

Archdeacon Farrar is another example of high literary and moral endowments. He is one of the most scholarly, logical, and instructive preachers of the day. His discourses are clear, racy, carefully prepared, and delivered in the best of style.   I cannot say that I ever listened to a preacher who gave me more pleasure and instruction.

A poet should have large Ideality and Sublimity to give vividness, refinement, and grandeur to his conceptions; large Language, Individuality, Comparison, Human Nature, and Constructiveness, with a good development of the other intellectual and moral organs.

A journalist requires Language, Eventuality, Mirthfulness, Comparison, Self-esteem, Friendship, and both energy and patience.

Fig. 8—W. M. Thackeray.

The novelist needs large perceptive organs, a good memory, descriptive power, imagination, and as many other good qualities as can be found in a human being.   The country is to-day flooded with trashy literature, which is the product of imperfect minds.   The novelist should be a good man, an intellectual man, and a cultivated man, with as much knowledge of the world as can be acquired. Many novels of to-day are written by men and women whh have cloistered themselves up with musty old books,

Fig. 9—M. Chatrian.

and who know nothing of the world and its ways, save what they have acquired through reading. Good literature should be the fruit of a healthy mind, which can only result from natural habits of observation and a sound body. The portraits that accompany these explanations will assist parents in ascertaining the abilities of their sons and daughters. They represent celebrated authors.

CHAPTER X.

PROFESSIONAL VOCATIONS.

GENERALLY speaking, the pursuits mentioned in the last chapter are included in the professions, and it may be difficult to distinguish the difference between them and those of this chapter; but the vocations mentioned here have reference mainly to money making, while poets, novelists, and clergymen very seldom make money. Good novelists generally make more for the publisher, after the death of the writer, than they made for themselves during their lifetime. And, perhaps, no poet in the world ever became rich, if we except the Poet Laureate, while lawyers, doctors, musicians, etc., etc., frequently become very wealthy and influential men; hence the difference that we have made.

For the pursuits mentioned in this chapter men should be strong both physically and mentally. There should be a more liberal development of the Physical Temperaments than in the case of the clergyman, but in other respects there need not be much difference. The musician, whether a singer or player, needs the Mental-Vital Temperament to give intensity and pathos, large social affections and Benevolence, to give sympathy and feeling, large Time,

Language, and Eventuality, and, in playing, large Constructiveness, and Locality, with full Combativeness and Self-Esteem. Gounôd illustrates this combination.

The Lawyer has much to do with the peace and friendship of the community, and therefore should be healthy, strong, and well balanced: his work is very exhausting,

Fig. 10—Gounod.

and requires a vigorous physiology. It also requires a great deal of mental culture, so that the intellectual faculties should be in the ascendancy, the executive or energising powers coming next; he should have large Language to give readiness, and good expression; he also needs firmness, independence, and a high moral nature; indeed, the lawyer should be a man, every inch of him, inside or out, and a good man too. The late Earl Cairns, whose portrait is here given, was one of the most successful lawyers that ever lived ; he possessed a high moral nature, and was a good practical Christian.   The portrait of Sir W. Vernon Harcourt illustrates the developments required in this vocation.

Fig. 11—The late Earl Cairns.

The doctor should be endowed with a harmonious organization, good health, an ample degree of the Vital Temperament to give recuperative energy, cheerfulness, ardour, joyousness, and a good magnetic influence.   He should have large perceptives to give a world of know-ledge of a practical character, a good memory, and strong reasoning faculties. He should be social and warm-hearted, firm and self-reliant, forcible and courageous, prudent and discreet, hopeful and witty, a good mechanic to perform surgical operations, he should have a high moral nature, and lastly, he should be religious.

The phrenologist really ought to have a first rate head, because he has to deal with and judge of every organ, faculty, and affection of the human body. Those phrenologists who are defective are liable to give imperfect delineations of character, and are incapable of giving sound

Fig. 12—Sir **W. V. Harcourt.**

advice. The advice a man gives always partakes largely of his own characteristics. In this pursuit a man should at least possess good perceptives, an excellent memory, large Comparison, and Human Nature, a full social development, and a high moral nature. The more refinement and ingenuity, freedom of expression, and culture he possesses, the better.

One great authority says :—" The phrenologist requires a temperament of the highest order, exceedingly quick yet strong, to impart both mental activity and power, and enable him to run rapidly, yet correctly, through the vast multiplicity of conditions which go to form character ; great strength of organization, to apply his entire energies with great power to the work in hand ; an ample intellectual lobe, to give power of mind, and, in connection with the required activity, to impart cogency, pointedness, efficiency, and distinctness ; an evenly-balanced intellect, so that he may take into full account all those conditions which influence character and conduct ; great Observation, so that he may perceive those conditions at a glance, and see all that can influence his ultimate conclusions ; ample Eventuality, to remember all he observes ; great Comparison, to combine and comprehend all the relative sizes of all the organs with each other, and with the existing temperament—a truly Herculean labour, and one which requires the utmost tension of this faculty ; a copious flow of Language, to facilitate description, and convey the results arrived at; good Mirth, to spice the whole with the lively and exciting ; good Causality, to investigate and present the great principles and general bearings of its philosophy ; not too much Secretion, lest he become ambiguous and avoid direct declarations ; large Parental Love, to gain him the good-will of those children he may be called upon to examine, so as to render his advice acceptable and dispose them to follow it ; large Kindness,.

thoroughly to interest him in the welfare of his patrons, and impart advice wherever required ; as well as to apply this science to human improvement and happiness ; and a high coronal region, so as to inspire him with high moral feelings and give all he says and does an elevated moral aspect, together with the strictest sense of justice and a well-balanced head, especially intellect ; because as he is, so will be his examinations and views. Predominant Causality and deficient Individuality render him too slow in arriving at conclusions ; yet this organization is not incompatible with his making excellent examinations, provided the required time is taken."

Statesmen require a Temperament that will give heart, solidity, and strength of mind, and a large and well-balanced intellectual lobe, to enable them to see through public measures, and choose the best course to be pursued. Their heads should not be as broad as those of business men, otherwise they will become self-interested, and seek selfish emolument rather than the public good ; nor should the head be too narrow, or they may become extravagant with the public money. Few callings require better men and more real philanthropy, yet few callings are so poorly supplied with such. The public in this country choose their representatives for the House of Commons from among the rich. The aristocracy, on account of their riches, are popular with the wealthy electors, and become M.P.'s. The people very seldom ask themselves the question : " Has this man capacity to formulate good laws, and to help manage successfully the affairs of the country?" It would be better for each country if its statesmen were liberally paid for their services, and encouraged to do their best for

Fig. 13—William Ewart Gladstone.

the interests of the people. The Right Hon. William Ewart Gladstone is a good illustration of the model statesman, both in physiology and intellect ; and, so far as I am able to judge, his moral nature is unimpeachable.

CHAPTER XI.

ARTISTIC WORK.

ARTISTS of all kinds require a highly organized Temperament, an exquisitely fine and active organization, as well as a pure and lofty one. The Mental-Vital Temperament is most favourable, together with a large development of Form, Size. Imitation, Constructiveness, and Ideality, to enable them to draw and copy nature, and also to impart taste and finish to their productions. The painter requires a predominance of the faculty of Colour, to enable him to judge of, mix, and apply colours with accuracy and beauty. Large Mirthfulness and Language to enable him to amuse and entertain his customers, and thus give them a pleasant expression of countenance when they sit for their portraits; large Imitation to render their portraits life like, and especially large Ideality, to give exquisiteness and elegance to both the colouring and entire picture.

A sculptor, as also a wood engraver, requires an organization similar to the painter, with perhaps a more liberal mixture of the Motive Temperament, and with large Firmness, Combativeness, and Destructiveness, to give vigour to their productions.

The photographer needs a Mental-Vital Temperament,

large perceptives, Constructivenes, Comparison, Ideality,
Language, and Mirthfulness, with a full degree of Friendship, and the social faculties generally. Colour is not so
indispensable in the photographer as in the case of the
painter, because he has not much to do with colour.
Sometimes he colours his photographs, in which case he
will need it as much as the painter.

Fig. 14—Rubens.

The accompanying portrait of Rubens is a good illustration of the successful artist. The face is a very fine
one ; the perceptives, Constructiveness, and Ideality are
large, and the intellectual faculties generally well developed.
The Temperament is exquisite, there being a predominance
of the Mental, with the Vital coming next, and the Motive
last.

D

CHAPTER XII.

CONDITIONS ESSENTIAL TO SUCCESS.

AFTER a person has entered upon a vocation for which he is by nature adapted, it will not do for him to fold his arms and hope for success. There are certain conditions essential to success, with which every man must comply before he can expect to succeed.

The first condition is good health. Many young men think they are doing a clever thing when, by excessive toil and early and late hours, they do the work of two persons, perhaps sparing the expense of a clerk in their business. You can see them going home late at night with books under their arms. These they do up instead of going to bed. The result is they lose their sleep, their mental faculties are impaired, the body is imperfectly nourished, and, at last, the health breaks down altogether.

I know a man who made, in business, twenty-six thousand pounds in sixteen years. He had a number of shops, all of which he superintended himself. The work was too much for him, and at length his health gave way. All his shops were left without his supervision and inspiration ; things went wrong for want of his assistance, and in the course of a few years he filed his petition in bankruptcy, and paid a few shillings to the pound on a large sum. While his health was good, he made money ; when his health failed, he began to lose it, until he was bankrupt.

I cannot here tell business men what they should do to preserve their health, but they will find all necessary information on this subject in " Body, Brain, and Mind," which I commend to their perusal.

Honesty is another condition of success. I quite agree that many men who are dishonest acquire property, but I never saw any such individuals enjoying the fruits of their deception. I have heard a man say to another, " He is too honest ; he will never get on." But this is a mistake. I know men who are truthful and upright in all their dealings, that have been remarkably successful, and who can enjoy their acquisitions conscious of their having been righteously gained. Moreover, if people discover a business man telling them lies, they cannot trust him, nor will they patronise him thereafter. Some time ago I was in the habit of spending several hundreds of pounds annually with a man in business. I discovered him telling me untruths, and have never spent a penny with him since. I believe that great numbers of people will do the same thing with men whom they discover practising deception. Therefore, though honesty is no policy at all, it will undoubtedly pay all men best to practise it.

Enthusiasm is another condition of success. Here we see the necessity of following a pursuit that harmonises with our consciences.   It is very difficult for us to sell an article of which we have an imperfect knowledge, and doubly so if we have but an indifferent opinion of it. A commercial traveller cannot enthusiastically represent a man in whom he has little confidence himself.   Nor can we successfully prosecute a trade that is opposed to our conception of right.   If we are working at something which will not only benefit ourselves, but also prove useful to other people, and no harm to anyone, then we can throw our whole heart and soul into the work and thus make it successful.

Industry is, of course, another condition of success.   Sir Robert Peel said: "Self help alone makes a man successful."   Into whatever line of accomplishment we turn our attention we see that persons occupying conspicuous positions have had to work very hard to acquire them.   "Good luck" always means hard work, and those men who have been most successful in life have been the hardest workers.   Lord Eldon was the son of a publican in Newcastle.   His father, though in a humble sphere of life, was able to give his sons a liberal education, but this particular son was very refractory, and it was supposed that he would never make anything worth a good education, so he was kept at home with his father.   Writing one day to his eldest son he said : " I don't know what to do with Jack ; he is beyond my management."   In reply, his son requested him to " send Jack to Oxford;" and he promised to see after him and do what he could for him.

Acting on this advice, his father sent him to college, where he stayed one term. During the vacation he spent his holidays in Newcastle, where he fell in love with a beautiful but poor girl, and married her contrary to his father's wishes. This act caused a rupture between father and son, and resulted in their separation. Securing what sustenance he could from his friends, he went to London and entered himself a student of the Middle Temple in 1773, and took his degree of Master of Arts in the following year. During his studies he lived in very poor apartments, and was, at one time, in a garret living on the meanest of fare. He rose early in the morning and studied late into the night, tying a damp towel round his head to keep him awake. He frequently found himself looking off the books, his brain seeming to seek rest involuntarily; and, to prevent this, he wrote in large letters on a sheet of paper the words— "Read or starve," and pinned it up above where he sat to read. After this, when he looked up, he saw the sheet, and, being reminded of the necessity of prosecuting his studies, he resolutely turned to his books. When he took his degree of M.A., he was twenty-three years of age. In the ordinary course he was called to the Bar, but his first year's earnings did not amount to twenty shillings. After patient and laborious study he rose into notice, and in 1783 was returned M.P. for Weobley. In 1787 he was appointed Chancellor of the Bishopric of the County Palatine of Durham, and, in the following year, Solicitor-General. In 1793 he was made Attorney-General, and in 1799 was raised to the Chief Justiceship of the Common Pleas, with a seat in the House of Lords as Baron Eldon. In 1801 he became Lord Chancellor of England. Thus we see that he rose from a very mean origin, and, step by step, filled important offices, until, at the age of 50, he occupied one of the highest offices in the State.

Lord Beaconsfield is another example of great success, arising from industry and persistent effort. He was the son of Isaac Disraeli, an English author of moderately liberal means. He was educated in a private school, and then placed in an attorney's office, where he continued for some time as a preparation for an appointment in a government office, which he did not obtain. At the age of twenty-one he became a contributor to a paper which lived only five months; but it seems to have had some effect upon his mind in after years, in so far as to give it a political bias. At the age of twenty-three he published his novel of " Vivian Grey," which was succeeded at various times by " Contarini Fleming," the " Young Duke," and several other works. While actively engaged in literary work he was continually before the public as a politician. At the age of twenty-six he stood for the representation of the borough of Wycombe, in the interest of the radical reforming party. He was unsuccessful, but nothing daunted, two years later he came forward in the same interest as a candidate for Marylebone. Again he was unsuccessful. Having failed as a radical, he came forward as a conservative candidate for the borough of Taunton,

but was here unsuccessful.   At the age of 32, as a conservative, he was returned member for Maidstone.   His
first speech in the House of Commons was like his first
attempts at political representation.   The effort was a
complete failure.   His speech was laughed at throughout,
and he was compelled to sit down before he had finished.
This however he did not do until he had said, "I have
begun several times many things, and often have succeeded
at last.   I shall sit down now, but the time will come when
you will hear me."   These words proved prophetic.   The
time came when he was listened to with the most anxious
interest.   At the age of thirty-six he was recognised as
the leader of the "Young England Party."   At 41 his
attacks upon Sir Robert Peel were as frequent as they
were often brilliant and severe.   At 47 he became
Chancellor of the Exchequer, under Lord Derby, and step
by step rose to the very highest position that could be
occupied by an Englishman, with the whole wealth of the
empire at his disposal.

Faraday, the great natural philosopher, was the son of
a blacksmith.   When a young man, he wrote to Sir H.
Davy, asking for employment at the Royal Institution.
Sir H. Davy consulted a friend on the matter.   "Here is a
letter from a young man named Faraday; he has been
attending my lectures, and wants me to give him employment at the Royal Institution.   What can I do?"   "Do?
Put him to wash bottles.   If he is good for anything he
will do it directly; if he refuses he is good for nothing."

Faraday did wash bottles, and his name now ranks amongst the most illustrious of the Victorian Era. He was of the same opinion as the poet who said :—

> " If I were a cobbler, I'd make it my pride
> *The best* old cobbler to be ;
> If I were a tinker, no tinker beside
> Should mend an old kettle like me.

"Whatsoever thy hand findeth to do, do it with thy might; " and I would add to them good old George Herbert's advice to the earnestly ambitious :—

> " Sink not in spirit ; who aimeth at the sky,
> Shoots higher much than he that means a tree."

Practical is the counsel of a modern bard, who writes :—

> " Do what you can, being what you are,
> Shine like a glow-worm, if not like a star,
> Work as a pulley, if not as a crane,
> Be a wheel-greaser, if you can't drive a train."

Numerous other examples similar to the above might be given, but it is unnecessary, to occupy more space, inasmuch as every observing person must see that success means hard work. I have met many young ladies ambitious to become musicians, but who would not work hard enough to gain success. All who have ever accomplished much in politics, business, literature, music, art, or anything else, have had to work hard. And so must all my readers who are ambitious to become distinguished. Nothing can be done without it.

CHAPTER XIII.

HOW TO SAVE MONEY.

MOST people would like to know how to save money, and it is right for every one to do so, for, if we live to be old, we shall not be able to work for ourselves, nor shall we wish to be dependent upon others. We come in contact with some people who, through ignorance, have placed themselves in circumstances where they cannot possibly save money.

Not long ago I fell into conversation with a man who had nine children, and was earning only eighteen shillings per week. I talked to him about the sin of having so many children, without sufficient means to support them, and he said, " It is God's will, and how am I to avoid it?" But, I say: "No! It is not God's will. Every man has the power to regulate the number of his own offspring."

The following case came under my notice at Easter, a year ago, while accompanying a friend, who was distributing oranges and pennies among the poor of a district in Carlisle. He called at the poor, dirty-looking cottage of a man whose boy attended the mission school, but had been absent for some weeks. The inside of the house looked very poverty-stricken ; the floor was bare, one table stood in the room, and all the seats, which were mainly stools and old boxes, were occupied by less than half the family, the others were sitting on the floor or standing about. The reason for the boy's absence was obvious enough—his clothing was insufficient to cover him. From a conversation with the father, the following facts were gathered :— There were eleven children, the wife, and himself. The eldest child was thirteen. No one in the house earned a penny but himself. He worked at Mr. ———'s brewery, and received 13/- per week, and as much beer as he could drink. He paid 2/9 per week for rent, and had to find firing, lights, food, clothing, and all the other necessaries of life for the whole family out of 13/-. If we take the rent off his wage it leaves 10/3, which is equal to a little less than 9½d. per week for each member of the family, or considerably under 1½d. a day. I know another man who has had twenty-one children, and never earned more than twenty shillings per week. To this class of men I have something to say in my work on " Man's Sexual Relations." I heartily sympathise with them and recommend them to study that work. To you who have not yet committed such an error, I would say : " Have no more children than you can easily support." Think seriously about this matter, and see if you cannot in some way obviate the direful consequences of a too numerous progeny. After this, exercise economy in everything. The wife or mistress of the household should exercise economy in carrying it on, especially with regard to food.

Dr. Nichols writes a book on " How to Live on Sixpence

a Day," but I can tell you how to live on threepence a day, and be strong and healthy. It will be necessary to live on grain, vegetables, and fruit. Have for breakfast wheat meal porridge or mush, brown bread and butter or cheese, with a little stewed fruit, or milk and sugar, to the mush. For dinner, baked potatoes, well boiled peas, beans, lentils, rice, tapioca, or any of the higher class of vegetables, with brown bread and cooked fruit, say apples, pears, plums, cherries, gooseberries, strawberries, prunes, or dates. For tea, take no tea whatever, but some bread and butter, and cocoa or milk, with a little fruit. This is a plain, palatable, healthy, nutritious, and cheap diet. I have tried it well, and proved it to be the best that I can have. If people use flesh meat it will cost them four times as much. Such articles as tobacco, snuff, spirits, wine, beer, pepper, mustard, vinegar, cinnamon, nutmeg, all-spices, rich pastry, pills, patent medicines, and stimulants of every kind, are expensive, useless, and injurious, and therefore ought never to be brought into a house, not mentioning a stomach. Then again, fine clothing (I don't mean substantial clothing, but finery), and jewellery, are useless and expensive luxuries, and may be, without any sacrifice, dispensed with. If men would live well, but plainly ; dress well, but with a view to comfort and economy ; utilize all their spare moments, abstain from the use of tobacco, snuff, and alcoholic drinks, and keep in mind that, although their wants may appear many, their real needs are few, they would save money, though their salary were small. And what is

more, and I think of the greatest value, is that this very
principle of economy would make them better men and
women.   Especially do we disapprove of much flesh meat;
in fact, I am disposed to think that God never intended
men to eat the flesh of their fellow-creatures.   If He
intended men to devour flesh, why did He not give them
tusks like other carnivora?   Why did He endow them
with benevolence or sympathy?   The most striking pecu-
liarity of carnivorous animals is their rapacity and ferocity.
The constitutional effect of animal food is to excite or
inflame Destructiveness—to generate cruelty; or, in other
words, the diet of carnivorous animals excites that cruelty
which enables them to devour their innocent prey.   If they
had a faculty of Benevolence, or the least spark of sympathy in them, they could not do it.   Nor can men kill
animals and eat them without perverting their Destructiveness, and crucifying the most Christ-like quality they
possess, viz., Benevolence.   That a flesh diet inflames Destructiveness in man is proved by the history of all savage,
warlike, and bloodthirsty nations and individuals.   The
uncivilized American Indian, who subsists largely on flesh,
is noted for his savage ferocity—his unrelenting revenge.
Like a fiend he exultingly inflicts the most excruciating
cruelties his tiger-like and inhuman nature can suggest.
Nowhere in history can we find a people noted for their
peaceable and amiable disposition, whose diet consisted
largely of flesh meat.   At the present time those nations
who eat flesh are most destructive and warlike.   Go back

to the Bible, and take for example the Jews. They were almost continually steeped in war, and slew men by the thousand ; even their women sang songs to this effect :— " Saul has slain his thousands, but David hath slain his tens of thousands."

It may be said that the English are a peaceful nation, and yet consume millions of carcases of beef and mutton every year. But the English are not peaceful. Our soldiers are almost continually busy. We may have peace at home, but at the very moment I write these words we are waging a bloody war in Egypt, and we have just finished a war with the Zulus. Before it commenced we were busy with the Afghans. Nay, I might go back for a hundred years and find no peace, but war and bloodshed, the work of inflamed Destructiveness.

Men who live mostly on flesh meat are most destructive, and least moral and amiable in disposition, while a farinaceous, vegetable, and fruit diet are promotive of goodness, gentleness, a kind, tender, generous, loving, and amiable disposition. If you live upon it, it will make you more a man, and less a savage, or a brute, and more Christ like.

Now, a man who is healthy in the broadest meaning of the word, is truly wealthy, is rich indeed. A man who enjoys perfect digestion, a vigorous circulation, uniform perspiration, healthy secretion, sound and unimpaired nervous action, easy locomotion, and a harmonious exercise of all the mental faculties,—when the action of all the faculties of the mind, and the functions of the entire corporeal system confer pleasure—then is that man rich indeed, and much to be envied by nine-tenths of the human race. To make life a pleasure, and turn everything into a source of enjoyment, we have but to obey the laws of God, and it is much easier to obey them than it is to break them. We have to exercise every part of the body in accordance with the governing law, or as primarily intended. These I cannot attempt to explain here, but I trust that what has been said will induce some to stop and think before they make any great mistake ; and if this book be the means of leading any into a better path of life, it will amply repay the labour spent in writing it.

APPENDIX.

Since publishing the first edition of this book, it has been pointed out to me that a " Symbolic Head," showing the location of all the phrenological organs, with a definition of the faculties, and also a few words of explanation relating to the temperaments were very much needed to enable readers to understand my remarks clearly, so in this edition I have included what was thought necessary.

When we use the word " Temperament," we refer to the predominance of some part of the physical constitution, as for instance the bones and muscles ; the stomach, liver, lungs, etc.; and the nerves.

We divide the Temperaments into three, and name them Motive, Mental, and Vital.

The Motive Temperament embraces the foundation, or frame work and moving powers of the body, viz., the bones and muscles. When these predominate, they give roughness and angularity to the features, combined with strength and endurance to the constitution. Persons in whom this Temperament is large are noted for their love of physical exercise, field sports, and sometimes hard work—for their untiring energy and indomitable perseverance. The accompanying engraving of Mr. Gladstone illustrates this Temperament.

The Vital Temperament includes all the internal visceral organs, or those parts whose function it is to create life force, such as the stomach, liver, lungs, intestines, etc. When these are large, the face will be round, the shoulders

Fig. 15.—William Ewart Gladstone.

broad, the chest and abdomen well developed, and all the limbs plump, round, and tapering. This condition gives enthusiasm, ardour, impulsiveness, and a whole-souled nature. John Bright is an illustrative example, as may be seen from his portrait.

The brain and nervous system, or that portion of the body through which mind is manifested, constitutes the Mental Temperament. When this is the most powerful part of the organization, the head is large, the forehead

Fig. 16—The late John Bright.

high and expanded, and the lower part of the face relatively small. The features are finely formed, and the body somewhat slender and delicate. This Temperament gives mind and susceptibility to mental impressions; it renders the conceptions vivid, the emotions intense, the thoughts quick, senses acute, and the imagination lively and brilliant. In Lord Beaconsfield this Temperament predominates over the other two, giving a decided tendency to a purely mental life.

Fig. 17—The late Earl Beaconsfield.

When the organization is harmonious in all its parts, there is harmony of the Temperaments and corresponding perfection of character.

A more lengthy treatment of the Temperaments will be found in the author's work on " Body, Brain, and Mind."

Advice will be found in that book for the cultivation or restraint of the Temperaments as the case may require. Each subject is illustrated with portraits of well-known individuals.

NATURAL LANGUAGE OF THE FACULTIES.

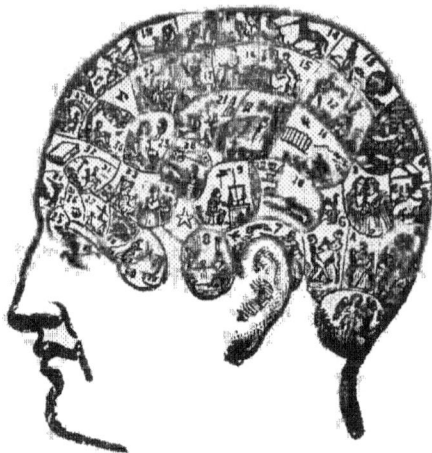

LOCATION OF THE ORGANS.

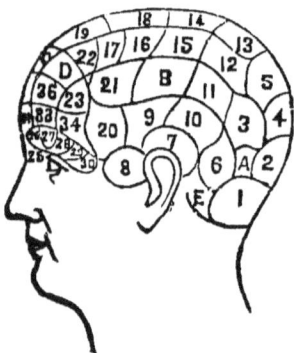

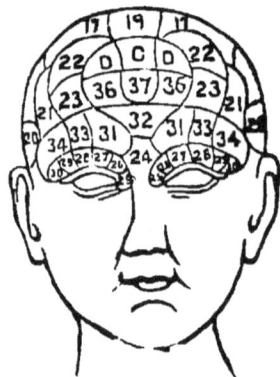

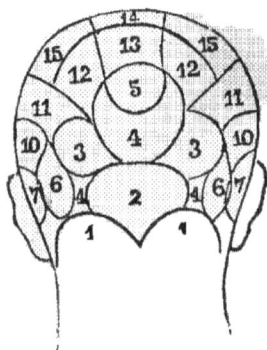

DEFINITION OF THE FACULTIES.

1. AMATIVENESS—Love of the Opposite Sex ; Desire to Caress, Kiss, and Fondle. *Excess*—Lust; Sensuality. *Deficiency*—Cold-heartedness; a want of Gallantry.

(*A*) CONJUGALITY — Attachment to One ; Desire to Marry ; Fidelity. *Excess*—Jealousy; Inordinate Attachment. *Deficiency*—Inconstancy ; Coquetry.

2. PARENTAL LOVE—Love of Children and Young Animals ; Desire for Offspring. *Excess*—Petting, Pampering, and Spoiling Children. *Deficiency*—Impatience with Children ; Neglect.

3. FRIENDSHIP—Love of Companions and Society ; Desire to Congregate ; Gregariousness. *Excess*—Indiscriminate attachment; Leads to Bad Company. *Deficiency* —Leads to Seclusion ; Cold-heartedness.

4. INHABITIVENESS—Love of Home ; Desire to live in one place; Love of Country ; Patriotism. *Excess*— Home Sickness; Indisposition to Travel. *Deficiency*—A Wandering Nature ; Neglect of Home.

(*E*) VITATIVENESS—Love of Life ; Power to Fight with Disease. *Excess*—Fear of Death. *Deficiency*— Desire for Death ; Yielding to Disease.

5. CONTINUITY—Concentrativeness; Application; One thing at once. *Excess*—Prolixity; Boring with tedious Iteration. *Deficiency*—Lack of Patience; Excessive Love of Change; Too many irons in the fire at once.

6. COMBATIVENESS—Spirit; Courage; Pluck; Boldness; Daring; Resolution. *Excess*—Contention; Irritability. *Deficiency* — Cowardice; Chicken-heartedness.

7. DESTRUCTIVENESS—Energy; Executiveness; Force; Resolution. *Excess*—Cruelty; Inhumanity; Malice; Hatred. *Deficiency*—Want of Energy; Easily overcome.

8. ALIMENTIVENESS—Appetite for Food; Gustatory Pleasure. *Excess*—Gluttony; Drunkenness. *Deficiency* —Poor Appetite; Neglect of Food.

9. ACQUISITIVENESS—Love of Money and Property; Desire to accumulate Wealth; Economy. *Excess*— Selfish, Miserly Disposition. *Deficiency*—Waste; Profusion; Extravagance.

10. SECRETIVENESS — Policy; Concealment; Tact; Strategy. *Excess*—Cunning; Deception; Trickery. *Deficiency*—Inability to Conceal one's Feelings, or Keep Secrets.

11. CAUTIOUSNESS—Guardedness; Anxiety; Prudence; Watchfulness. *Excess*—Indecision; Want of Promptitude; Procrastination; Fear. *Deficiency* Recklessness; Rashness; Carelessness; Want of Forethought.

12. APPROBATIVENESS—Ambition; Desire to please; Love of popularity; Politeness. *Excess* — Vanity; Superficial show; Affectation. *Deficiency*—Disregard for praise or popularity.

13. SELF-ESTEEM—Love of self; Dignity; Self confidence; Desire for Liberty and Independence. *Excess* —Conceit; Egotism; Tyranny; Haughtiness; Pride. *Deficiency* — Humility; Meanness; Want of self-respect.

14. FIRMNESS—Stability; Will Power; Perseverance; Decision. *Excess*—Obstinacy; Stupidity; Inflexibility. *Deficiency*—Fickleness; Want of Perseverance.

15. CONSCIENTIOUSNESS—Honesty; Justice; Integrity; Sense of Right. *Excess*—Undue self-condemnation; Censoriousness. *Deficiency*—Want of Integrity; Inconsistency.

16. HOPE—Expectation; Anticipation; Trust; Confidence in the future; Sense of Immortality. *Excess*—Unwise speculations; Careless promises; Castle Building. *Deficiency*—Melancholy; Despondency; Afraid to Venture.

17. SPIRITUALITY—Intuition; Wonder; Faith; Credulity; Belief in Providence. *Excess*—Superstition; Belief in Ghosts; Witchcraft. *Deficiency*—Scepticism; Materialism; Unbelief.

18. VENERATION—Devotion; Adoration of a Supreme Being; Sense of Holiness; Reverence of things Sacred; Respect for the Aged. *Excess*—Idolatry; Bigotry; Superstitions. *Deficiency*—Disrespect and neglect of the old; Irreverence.

19. BENEVOLENCE—Sympathy; Kindness; Generosity; Philanthropy; Tenderness. *Excess*—Injudicious liberality; Prodigality in giving. *Deficiency*—Selfishness; Inhumanity.

20. CONSTRUCTIVENESS—Mechanical skill; Ingenuity; Dexterity; Versatility of Talent. *Excess* — Wastes Time and Money on Perpetual Motion. *Deficiency* —Inability to use tools or understand machinery.

21. IDEALITY—Refinement; Purity of Feeling; Love of Poetry and Art; Expansiveness of Mind. *Excess*— Fastidiousness; Too much love for finery. *Deficiency*— Want of Taste and Style; Want of Refinement; Unpolished.

(B) SUBLIMITY—Perception and Love of the Grand, Illimitable, Omnipotent, and Infinite; Love of the Wild and Terrific. *Excess* — Bombast; Excessive Show. *Deficiency*—Inability to appreciate the Sublime, Gorgeous, and Magnificent.

22. IMITATION—Ability and Disposition to copy, take Pattern, and Mimic; Versatility of Manner. *Excess* —

Buffoonery ; Ridiculous Pranks ; Low and Vulgar Tricks. *Deficiency*—Cannot Copy ; Do everything in their own way.

23. MIRTHFULNESS—Sense of the Absurd ; Humour ; Fun ; Laughter. *Excess*—Making Fun of the Aged, and on serious occasions. *Deficiency*—A Lack of Wit ; Gravity.

24. INDIVIDUALITY—Observation ; Desire to see and examine ; Minute examination. *Excess* — Curiosity ; Over Inquisitive. *Deficiency*—Superficial Examination.

25. FORM—Memory for Faces, Shape, and Outline ; Ability to Draw. *Excess*—Sees Ghosts, etc. *Deficiency* —Inability to Recognise Persons and Things.

26. SIZE—Cognizance of Bulk ; Quantity ; Magnitude, etc. ; Eye Measuring Power. *Excess*—Pained by Disproportion. *Deficiency* — Poor Judgment of Size, Quantity, Distance, etc. ; Inability to measure with the Eye.

27. WEIGHT—Sense of Gravity, Force, and Resistance ; Power to Balance the Body, etc. *Excess*—Unreasonable Venture in Dangerous Places. *Deficiency*—A Want of Balancing Power.

28. COLOUR — Appreciation of Colours ; Power to Arrange and Combine them. *Excess*—Too great Love for Gaudy Colours. *Deficiency*—Colour Blindness.

29. ORDER—Method; System; Arrangement; Neatness. *Excess*—Pained by Disorder. *Deficiency*—Carelessness; Slovenliness.

30. CALCULATION — Memory for Numbers; Mental Arithmetic; Quickness in Making Estimates. *Excess*— Are apt to neglect other things for Statistical Information. *Deficiency*—Incorrect in Using Figures.

31. LOCALITY—Cognizance of Places; Desire to Travel; Talent for Geography and Navigation. *Excess*—Roving Cosmopolitan Disposition. *Deficiency* — Forgets Places and Localities; Cannot find one's way.

32. EVENTUALITY—Memory of Facts; Circumstances; Stories; News; History; Biography. *Deficiency*— Inability to Remember Facts, etc.

33. TIME—Punctuality; Memory for Dates; Sense of Duration. *Deficiency*—Forgets when things occurred; Non-Punctuality.

34. TUNE—Sense of Melody; Love of Music; Memory for Tunes. *Excess*—Neglects the Duties of Life to gratify the Love of Music. *Deficiency*—Inability to Sing or Modulate the Voice in Reading or Speaking.

35. LANGUAGE—Memory for words; Ability to Communicate one's Thoughts. *Excess*—Verbosity; Loquacity. *Deficiency*—Inability to Express one's Thoughts Freely; Hesitancy of Speech.

36. CAUSALITY—Originality of Thought; Power to Think, Plan, Invent, Contrive, Philosophise, Argue, Reason, etc. *Excess*—Leads to Impracticable Theories. *Deficiency*—Inability to Plan, etc.; Shallow-mindedness.

37. COMPARISON—Sense of Resemblance; Criticism; Power to Compare, Analyse, Classify, Draw Inferences, etc. *Excess*—Undue Criticism. *Deficiency*—Inability to Illustrate and Apply Knowledge.

(C) HUMAN NATURE—Power to Read Character; Sagacity; Penetration. *Excess*—Suspicion, Prognostication. *Deficiency*—Inability to Read Motive and Disposition.

(D) AGREEABLENESS—Blandness; Affability; Persuasiveness; Ability to Interest and Entertain others. *Excess*—Affectation. *Deficiency* — Bluntness; Inadaptation of Deportment.